BILBAO

THE CITY AT A GLAN

GW00835843

Teatro Arriaga

Inspired by the Théâtre de la
in Paris, Joaquín Rucoba's 1890
has suffered drama of its own
fires. Renovation in 1986 resto
See p009

Estación de Santander

Severino Achúcarro's colourful art nouveau
façade to this 1902 station boasts decorative
window grilles, light fixtures and stonework,
epitomising the optimism of the era.
Bailén 2

Torre BBVA

This 88m bank tower, designed by Jaime Torres,
Enrique Casanueva and José María Chapa, was
the city's tallest building for 41 years. Bands
of tinted windows reflect a soothing pink sheen.
See p009

Plaza Moyúa

The modern city radiates from this point, home
to the regal Hotel Carlton (see p016) since 1926.

Isozaki Atea

Japanese architect Arata Isozaki's 'Gate' to
Bilbao is defined by a pair of 82m towers, with
interlocked buildings leading off at angles.
See p015

Torre Iberdrola

Sticking out like a particularly sore thumb
in this low-rise city, Cesar Pelli's tower has
been visible from almost any point since 2010.
See p014

Arcos Rojos

Daniel Buren's sculpture was created for the
10th anniversary of the Guggenheim (see p012)
and crowns the Puente de La Salve. Lights
lining its underbelly guide the way at night.

INTRODUCTION
THE CHANGING FACE OF THE URBAN SCENE

You'll have heard about the Guggenheim, seen photos no doubt, and it might well be the sole reason for your visit to Bilbao. Yet when you emerge from a tunnel onto the Puente de La Salve high above the Nervión River, and you see the museum glinting below, it still takes your breath away. The stagnation of the shipbuilding and steel industries had led to the city's former nickname, *El Botxo* (The Hole). But the Bilbaínos came up with an ambitious plan in the shape of Frank Gehry's masterpiece, which sparked a tourist boom as well as widespread regeneration. It sired a global phenomenon, with cities the world over attempting to emulate the 'Bilbao Effect', which here has led to further statement buildings and projects by architects including Lord Foster, Philippe Starck, Rafael Moneo, Santiago Calatrava, Cesar Pelli, Richard Rogers and Zaha Hadid.

If you first make the city's acquaintance for its architecture and art, the reason for your return will be the food. Epicurean delights and Michelin stars await throughout the Basque country, not least in neighbouring San Sebastián. The seaside resort is an art nouveau gem, with myriad belle époque façades, and we have included it in this guide because, well, it would have been rude not to. But this is Bilbao's time. Spain's fifth largest city deserves to be taken seriously, its industrial past no longer an albatross around its neck, the river once again its lifeblood. The good ship Bilbao has set sail, and it's time to swing the champagne and catch a ride.

ESSENTIAL INFO
FACTS, FIGURES AND USEFUL ADDRESSES

TOURIST OFFICE
Plaza Ensanche 11
T 94 479 5760
www.bilbao.net

TRANSPORT
Car hire
Avis
T 94 427 5760
www.avis.com
Europcar
T 94 423 9390
www.europcar.com
Metro
T 94 425 4000
www.metrobilbao.net
Trains run from around 6am until 11pm
Taxis
Radio Taxi
T 94 444 8888
Tele Taxi
T 94 410 2121
There are various cab ranks in the centre

EMERGENCY SERVICES
Emergencies
T 112
Late-night pharmacy
Check the rota in your local
pharmacy window

EMBASSIES/CONSULATES
British Consulate
8th floor
Alameda Urquijo 2
T 94 415 7722
www.ukinspain.fco.gov.uk
US Embassy
Serrano 75
Madrid
T 91 587 2200
madrid.usembassy.gov

MONEY
American Express
La Rambla 74
Barcelona
T 93 342 7311
www.americanexpress.com

POSTAL SERVICES
Post office
Alameda Urquijo 19
T 94 470 9336
Shipping
Mail Boxes Etc
Virgen de Begoña 47
T 94 435 2114

BOOKS
The Basque Country: A Cultural History
by Paddy Woodworth (Signal Books)
The Basque History of the World
by Mark Kurlansky (Vintage)
Obabakoak by Bernardo Atxaga (Vintage)

WEBSITES
Architecture
www.bilbaoenconstruccion.nireblog.com
Art
www.bilbaoarte.org
Newspaper
www.elcorreo.com

COST OF LIVING
Taxi from Sondika Airport to city centre
€24
Cappuccino
€1.80
Packet of cigarettes
€3.75
Daily newspaper
€1.20
Bottle of champagne
€55

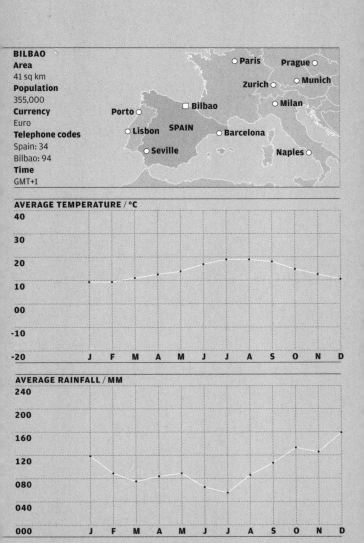

BILBAO
Area
41 sq km
Population
355,000
Currency
Euro
Telephone codes
Spain: 34
Bilbao: 94
Time
GMT+1

Paris · Prague ·
Zurich · · Munich
Porto · □ Bilbao · Milan
· Lisbon SPAIN · Barcelona
· Seville Naples ·

AVERAGE TEMPERATURE / °C

40											
30											
20											
10											
00											
-10											
-20	J	F	M	A	M	J	J	A	S	O	N	D

AVERAGE RAINFALL / MM

240											
200											
160											
120											
080											
040											
000	J	F	M	A	M	J	J	A	S	O	N	D

NEIGHBOURHOODS
THE AREAS YOU NEED TO KNOW AND WHY

To help you navigate the city, we've chosen the most interesting districts (see below and the map inside the back cover) and colour-coded our featured venues, according to their location; those venues that are outside these areas are not coloured.

INDAUTXU

Historically home to the bourgeoisie, Indautxu boasts the city's most exclusive shops, along Rodríguez Arias and Ercilla, and hip late-night haunts on Simón Bolívar and Manuel Allende. The next stage of Bilbao's urban regeneration is taking place just north of here in Olabeaga.

CASCO VIEJO

The old town is an atmospheric warren of pedestrianised alleys centred around the neoclassical Plaza Nueva and the medieval Siete Calles (Seven Streets), which are a joy to get lost in. Now home to boutiques, bars and restaurants, it's a great backdrop for an early evening *pintxo* (tapas) crawl.

GETXO

A young, fashionable, beachside suburb dotted with 1920s villas at the mouth of the Nervión, Getxo is a 20-minute metro ride from Moyúa. The Puente Vizcaya (see p010) is a legacy of its industrial past, but these days the vibe is relaxed and the draw is purely recreational. The old fishing village of Algorta is a whitewashed delight.

ABANDOIBARRA

The docks on the west riverbank were ripped up to make way for the Guggenheim (see p012), Torre Iberdrola (see p014), Palacio Euskalduna (see p074) and Rafael Moneo's Biblioteca Universidad de Deusto (Avenida Abandoibarra). Linking them is a tramway and a sculpture-strewn promenade.

BILBAO LA VIEJA

For decades, this creative, bohemian enclave was a neglected area populated by North African immigrants, but designers and artists have now moved in, leading the local press to dub it *El Soho Bilbaíno*. The edgier nightlife kicks off here and there's a clutch of enticing restaurants.

ABANDO AND ENSANCHE

El Ensanche means 'the extension' and it was here that Bilbao spread from the Casco Viejo – the streets were laid out from 1876. The district is now the city's business hub dissected by the retail drag Gran Vía. There are plenty of after-work *pintxo* bars, especially along Ledesma.

MOYÚA

The area north of Bilbao's beating heart, Plaza Moyúa, has experienced the Guggenheim Effect most acutely. Here, the city's best hotels – the Gran Domine (see p017) and Miró (see p023) – and a profusion of galleries and well-designed bars and eateries have joined Bilbao's original art museum, the Bellas Artes (see p033).

MIRIBILLA

This suburb was created between 1999 and 2004, when 3,000 apartments were built on top of a former iron mine high above the city. If not for the views or the sports centre (see p088), it is worth visiting Miribilla to pay homage to IMB's sublime contemporary church (see p065).

LANDMARKS
THE SHAPE OF THE CITY SKYLINE

Small enough to explore on foot and easy to navigate, as befits its shipbuilding past, Bilbao is laid out with a sailor's shore leave in mind. The modern core is essentially circular, with eight streets radiating in a compass from Plaza Moyúa. The Nervión River hugs its circumference, its embankment no longer lined with clanking docks but, going upriver, now home to the Palacio Euskalduna (see p074), the Guggenheim (see p012) and Isozaki Atea (see p015). Round the bend, the Teatro Arriaga (Plaza Arriaga 1, T 94 479 2036) announces the densely packed old town, Casco Viejo. Across the water is the 1969 Torre BBVA (Plaza Circular), which marks Bilbao's financial heart. A little further along, the art deco Mercado de La Ribera (Ribera, T 94 415 7086), designed by Pedro Ispizua in 1929, has a lovely stained-glass window and was renovated for 2011.

Lolling hills hem the city in, so development funnelled along the 15km of river heading up to the coast. Here, the hard-working suburb of Portugalete sits on the west of the estuary, jealously eyeballing knockabout Getxo, the two joined by the iconic Puente Vizcaya (overleaf), a wonder of the industrial age. Back in town, the contemporary symbol of progress is Torre Iberdrola (see p014), which has given the skyline something of a wake-up call. Even if Bilbao's famous drizzle descends, bear in mind you're never more than a stroll from the Gugg, where often it seems all roads lead.
For full addresses, see Resources.

Puente Vizcaya

The 'Hanging Bridge' is an 1893 marvel. Its unique shuttle mechanism and steel-cable technology were used as a blueprint for bridge construction across the globe. Local designer Alberto Palacio and French engineer Ferdinand Arnodín's triumph across the mouth of the Nervión was designated a UNESCO World Heritage Site in 2006. To allow shipping access to the docks downstream, the actual 'bridge' (made with local iron) was built 45m above the water. Suspended at road level is a gondola that transports up to six vehicles and 200 people 24 hours a day, and there's a vertigo-inducing 160m walkway over the top with superb views (€5; 10am-sunset). Remarkably, aside from being sabotaged to hinder Franco's troops in the Spanish Civil War, the bridge has never stopped working. *T 94 480 1012, www.puente-colgante.com*

Guggenheim Museum

Frank Gehry's 1997 masterpiece was the catalyst for Bilbao's metamorphosis from industrial slug to cultural butterfly. A 2010 survey of top architects nominated it as the most important building constructed worldwide since 1980. It has been likened to everything from an artichoke to Marilyn Monroe's skirt, but we'll settle for a whale. The 0.38mm titanium 'fish-scale' skin plays with the sunlight; the building changes perspective like an underwater refraction depending on your viewpoint; the entrance sucks you into its underbelly like Jonah; and its tail – stairs climbing an empty tower – wraps around Puente de La Salve, the entry point to Bilbao. We don't wish to diminish its jaw-dropping impact further with superlatives – go see for yourselves.
Avenida Abandoibarra 2, T 94 435 9000, www.guggenheim-bilbao.es

Torre Iberdrola

Cesar Pelli's tower for the Spanish energy company Iberdrola is impossible to ignore. At 165m, it's almost double the height of anything else in Bilbao. It dwarfs Isozaki Atea (opposite) and the Torre BBVA and makes an arresting statement clad in 4,800 glinting glass panels that reflect the surrounding hills. The undulating canopy entrance invites you in — but sadly the building is not open to the public.

Its pilot-light shape in cross-section could be a musing on the Iberdrola logo, although locals choose to believe it echoes the shield of beloved football team Athletic Bilbao (even though all football shields are the same shape). A pair of gently curving apartment blocks, designed by Carlos Ferrater, Luis Domínguez and Xavier Martí, finished in 2011, guard the tower's base. *Plaza Euskadi, www.torreiberdrola.es*

Puente Zubizuri and Isozaki Atea

Zubizuri means 'White Bridge' in Basque and Santiago Calatrava's playful, flapping sail blew into town in 1997. The footbridge's apparent weightlessness is emphasised by a glass-panelled walkway and it looks as if the whole thing might fly away in a strong breeze. In 2008, its sensuous curves were anchored architecturally by Isozaki Atea, designed by Arata Isozaki and local firm IA+B, although Calatrava objected to the modification to his work. The Atea complex comprises two glass-and-aluminium towers that flank the bridge, linked at unusual angles to blocks of green granite and red brick, with protruding volumes and cantilevered boxes. Public space is delineated within the preserved exterior walls of Gregorio Ibarreche's 1926 Depósito Franco customs warehouse.
Paseo Uribitarte

HOTELS

WHERE TO STAY AND WHICH ROOMS TO BOOK

In the years BG (Before Guggenheim), Bilbao wouldn't have known a boutique hotel if it had appeared each evening to turn down the beds. But today, the grandes dames Hotel López de Haro (see p020) and Hotel Carlton (Plaza Moyúa 2, T 94 416 2200), designed in 1919 by Manuel María de Smith and featuring a stunning glass cupola above its oval entrance hall, don't have it all their own way. Close to Gehry's museum and impressively designed themselves are the Gran Domine (opposite), the Miró (see p023) and, a little further on, the Meliá (Lehendakari Leizaola 29, T 94 428 0000), a project by Mexican architect Ricardo Legorreta with a typically colourful and monumental lobby of stone and marble. Top business choices include the Zenit (Autonomía 58, T 94 410 8108) and the Gran Ercilla (Ercilla 37, T 94 470 5700), which has a restaurant, Bermeo, lauded as one of the best hotel-dining experiences in Spain.

Perched on a hill 12km outside the city centre on the way to the airport (convenient if you have an early flight) is the gorgeous Palacio Urgoiti (see p026). Further inland, in the heart of Rioja country, Frank Gehry and Santiago Calatrava have gone head to head with wineries. Gehry's venture is also a hotel, the Marqués de Riscal (see p097), and includes many of his trademark touches, notably a flamboyantly sculptural titanium roof. There's no better spot to share a bottle of Finca Torrea than in its Rooftop Lounge. *For full addresses and room rates, see Resources.*

Gran Hotel Domine

When you arrive in Bilbao, the first thing you see is the Guggenheim. The second is local architects IA+B's 2002 hotel, which pays its respects to its neighbour with a broken mirror of a façade that reflects the museum like a cubist dream. Inside, a glass-roofed atrium (above) rising up all seven floors is dominated by a 26m pebble tower. Interiors, including this phallic sculpture, are by Estudio Mariscal, interspersed with Philippe Starck baths, Alvar Aalto stools, Arne Jacobsen taps and tributes to 20th-century design in the Bauhaus-inspired Café Metropol and 1960s-style Splash and Crash cocktail bar. Book one of the Club Rooms (overleaf) or a suite overlooking the museum. Breakfast on the roof terrace is a great start to the day.
Alameda Mazarredo 61, T 94 425 3300, www.granhoteldominebilbao.com

Guggenheim Club Room, Gran Hotel Domine

Hotel López de Haro
Named after the city's founder, Don Diego López de Haro V, the HLH has been a fixture of Bilbao social life since 1990. The décor is traditional with an English influence. Brass and darkwood furnishings, oak panelling, marble floors and heavy rugs and carpets abound in the public spaces, such as the clubby Ambigú Lounge bar (opposite). However, the Standard Rooms (above) have a more contemporary décor, courtesy of a 2007 revamp by local firm Zaila, featuring bold floral Osborne & Little wallpaper, stainless-steel and glass fittings and a monochrome colour scheme with splashes of red. There's a women-only floor, and wi-fi and flatscreen TVs throughout. The Basque and international cuisine in Club Náutico, with its checked floor, stained glass and sculpted steel, attracts the city's movers and shakers.
Obispo Orueta 2-4, T 94 423 5500, www.hotellopezdeharo.com

Hesperia

Designed by IA+B and dubbed the 'Hotel of Colours' for its tinted Vanceva windows, the Hesperia is a great budget option. The bar and restaurant are decorated with modern art and sculpture, while circular sofas and cowhide upholstery lend a quirky touch. The defining feature of the 151 rooms is that they are bathed in coloured light filtered through the windows, so the décor is pared down, featuring simple blondwood and pale linens. The best rooms are the double-aspect Junior Suites at the front of the hotel; the higher you are, the better the view. The Presidential Suite is a class above, and has an adjoining room for your bodyguard, a jacuzzi and a roof terrace on which to receive dignitaries. *Paseo Campo de Volantín 28, T 94 405 1100, www.hesperia-bilbao.es*

Hotel Miró

The perfectly integrated interiors of the city's only true boutique hotel are by the fashion designer Antonio Miró. The 50 rooms, such as the City Double (overleaf), have black Marquina marble bathrooms, partitioned off with cream drapes, and mod-cons including 32in flatscreen TVs and iHomes. Higher category rooms are more spacious, a feeling enhanced by huge windows, and decorated with an excellent photography collection including work by Ruud Van Empel and Ana Laura Aláez, as are the mezzanine/library (above) and the courtesy bar. There's a cute 85 sq m spa with a Japanese feel in the basement for private bookings; it's perfect for couples. If it's possible to scream understated style, that is exactly what the Miró does. *Alameda Mazarredo 77, T 94 661 1880, www.mirohotelbilbao.com*

City Double, Hotel Miró

Palacio Urgoiti
The 17th-century palace of Don José María Solano was rebuilt as a 43-room hotel on a hill above the city in 2005. Dismantled stone by stone from its original location in Galdakao 30 years ago to make way for the Bilbao-Behovia road, the reconstruction nearly didn't happen after floods in 1983 destroyed the warehouse where the stone, doors and blueprints were stored. The best room keys are for the three Junior Suites (opposite), which have colossal beds, antique furniture, balconies and marble bathrooms large enough for a party. There's also an indoor pool complete with a fountain, a gym and the Basque restaurant, Harria (meaning 'stone'). Those who've packed their argyle and plus fours are in for a treat, as there's a wonderfully located nine-hole pitch and putt course in the grounds, one of very few in Bilbao.
Arritugane, Mungia, T 94 674 6868,
www.palaciourgoiti.com

Hotel Embarcadero

Any thoughts of sailing off into the sunset from the seafront Hotel Embarcadero are dispelled as soon as you enter this neo-Basque villa set in landscaped gardens. Interiors, such as the Lounge (above), are decorated in a 1920s style. The 27 rooms are all well appointed, but we suggest you book either of the two suites with sea views, preferably the one with a balcony. Stay at the Embarcadero to enjoy the laidback vibe of Getxo, browse its fashion boutiques and dine on the day's catch in either Karola Etxea (T 94 460 0868) or Asador El Puerto-Zabala (T 94 491 2166), both set in creaky, timber-beamed fisherman's cottages in the charming village of Algorta. It's a 45-minute amble around the bay and then a steep climb. *Avenida Zugazarte 51, T 94 480 3100, www.hotelembarcadero.com*

Villa Soro, San Sebastián

Those who prefer privacy to the red carpet should eschew the celebrity haunt Maria Cristina when in San Sebastián and stay at Villa Soro, a tranquil hotel housed in a renovated 1898 mansion. Its location is not as convenient and there is no restaurant, but Arzak (see p054), one of Spain's culinary highlights, is 500m away, bike hire is free, the setting is delightful and the service is unparalleled. Opt for one of the 15 elegant rooms in the main villa; they're individually decorated, dappled in light and display local art and sculpture, including work by Jorge Oteiza. But it's the museum-piece public spaces that impress the most – the sitting rooms (opposite) furnished with antiques, the imposing staircase, the oak-panelled bar and the gardens by the 19th-century French landscape designer Pierre Ducasse.
Avenida de Ategorrieta 61, T 94 329 7970, www.villasoro.com

24 HOURS

SEE THE BEST OF THE CITY IN JUST ONE DAY

Study Bilbao's evolution with a constitutional along the river, from the Casco Viejo to the starchitecture. In fact, a stroll around any part of town throws up easy rewards, as Bilbao's character often varies from block to block – the compact centre is like a city-in-miniature.

The Guggenheim (see p012) is on every itinerary but the Museo de Bellas Artes (opposite) is another must-see, and the Alhóndiga (see p037) has become a focal point for locals. It's also a great option on a Sunday or Monday, when many other venues are closed. The siesta is observed too but shops open late, so put retail therapy on hold to enjoy a lazy lunch at Atea (see p034), La Gallina Ciega (see p047) or Baita Gaminiz (Alameda Mazarredo 20, T 94 424 2267), to sample Aitor Elizegi's modern Basque cuisine, preferably on the deck above the river. You'll soon realise food is essential to Basque life. Early evening, drop into any of the myriad tapas bars. Later, you're spoilt for choice with restaurants: El Perro Chico (see p042) and Etxanobe (see p074) are among Bilbao's most fêted.

For cocktails, head to the outdoor bar above Yandiola (see p057) or the tiny Antigua Cigarrería (Astarloa 5, T 94 424 8973). Locals only really let their hair down at weekends. Many a Bilbaíno night has segued into morning at Public Lounge (see p038), as well as megaclub Fever (Tellería 27, T 94 459 8617), where four rooms cater to all tastes in music. In fine Spanish tradition, it gets going at 3am. *For full addresses, see Resources.*

10.00 Museo de Bellas Artes

The Bellas Artes is oft overlooked, but it is one of Spain's top art museums. Breakfast in the café beside Parque de Doña Casilda Iturrizar before feasting on the 9,000-piece collection that stretches back to the 12th century; highlights include works by Francisco de Goya, Francis Bacon, El Greco and Basques Jorge Oteiza and Ignacio Zuloaga. Álvaro Líbano and Ricardo Beascoa's modernist extension was added to the neoclassical building in 1970 and the entire museum was redeveloped in 2001 by Luís María Uriarte. Temporary exhibitions often grab headlines, such as the Cristóbal Balenciaga retrospective (above) in 2010. Afterwards — oh, go on then — it's only a stroll to the Guggenheim, and you'll have avoided the morning rush.
Plaza Museo 2, T 94 439 6060, www.museobilbao.com

14.00 Atea

Chef Daniel García won a Michelin star at white-tablecloth institution Zortziko (T 94 423 9743) round the corner, but here he has ventured down a more populist path. Atea is a chilled-out contemporary bistro upriver from the Guggenheim on the ground floor of Isozaki Atea (see p015). The art nouveau iron grillwork survives over the windows, and rough walls have been left untouched. The airy interior, with spare, functional furnishings and a muted palette, was designed by local firm Q Diseño to contrast with the historic shell. The long white pine tables and extensive menu of *pintxos* and *raciones* – maybe baby squid *croquetas* or salmon and peach brochettes – invite sharing. A crate in the entrance is stamped 'Handle with Care', but you'll have no such worries about the cuisine, so don't be afraid to experiment. *Paseo Uribitarte 4, T 94 400 5869, www.atearestaurante.com*

16.00 Persuade

This absolute gem of a concept store is clearly a labour of love for owners Rosa Orrantia and Paul Ziarsolo, whose creative vision and personal approach have fostered a loyal international following. There's an eclectic mix of fashion and accessories from the likes of Dries Van Noten, Issey Miyake and Yohji Yamamoto alongside oriental antiques, 1950s and 1960s furniture, modern pieces by designers such as Christian Astuguevieille, and covetable items everywhere you look in this barn-like former pottery. The space was renovated in conjunction with Katsura Architects and features bare stone and brick walls, wooden rafters and a glass roof. Service is exceptional yet unfussy. Even if you don't buy anything, you'll leave happy.
Villarías 8, T 94 423 8864,
www.persuade.es

17.30 Alhóndiga

Ricardo de Bastida's 1909 modernista wine warehouse had languished empty since the 1970s until it underwent a theatrical makeover by Philippe Starck. It reopened in 2010 as a 43,000 sq m cultural complex. The original façade and cupolas remain largely intact, but the interior was gutted and replaced by three red-brick buildings supported by a forest of 43 low columns, each inspired by a historical decorative motif, and a vast atrium dimly lit by a virtual sun (above). There's always plenty going on here – the Alhóndiga hosts events and contains an exhibition space, a cinema, restaurants, a gym and a top-floor, glass-bottomed pool with a sun terrace (€5.80 entry). Starck's playful imprint even extends to the outsized street furniture. *Plaza Arriquibar 4, T 94 401 4014, www.alhondigabilbao.com*

21.30 Public Lounge

The maximalist, neo-gothic décor at this restaurant/bar is unlike anything else in the city, perhaps unlike anything outside the imagination of owner Patxi Ortún. Part medieval banquet, part vampiric boudoir, it is full of contemporary design and witty touches. In the window is a pink 'Flap' sofa by Francesco Binfarè lit by an art nouveau chandelier. Elsewhere are Jaime Hayon's 'Showtime' chair (opposite), framed stag antlers (found in the woods) draped with textiles, paintings by local artist Ignacio Goitia (above; all for sale) and a blood-red mosaic-tiled floor. Try the 48-hour Aranda lamb shoulder and something straight and strong from the bar, which specialises in spirits. At the weekend, tables are cleared for DJ sessions and dancing until dawn. *Henao 54, T 94 405 2824, www.public-bilbao.com*

URBAN LIFE
CAFÉS, RESTAURANTS, BARS AND NIGHTCLUBS

Even in its darkest years, Bilbao had one major pulling point – its cuisine, widely acknowledged as the best in Spain. In the 1970s, all-male gastronomy clubs, influenced by French nouvelle cuisine and Japanese and Asian techniques, reinvented traditional Basque dishes. The *nueva cocina vasca* movement has produced many sensational chefs – Juan Mari Arzak (see p054), Daniel García (see p034), Martín Berasategui (see p096) – and Michelin stars; San Sebastián alone has 14. Add the fact that you're in prime Rioja country, and you have the recipe for the best meal of your life.

Inventiveness is also to the fore in the Basque version of tapas: *pintxos*, bite-sized delicacies on baguette slices that adorn even the most unassuming bar counters. Do as the locals do and go for a post-work *txikiteo* (crawl), sampling each place's speciality, often cooked to order, be it turkey neck in filo or anchovies with sea urchin roe, washed down with miniature glasses of wine (*chatos*) or beer (*zuritos*). Just ignore the discarded toothpicks and napkins that litter the floor, and leave enough room for dinner.

Nightlife is undernourished in comparison – exquisite cuisine leaves little room for partying – apart from in arty La Vieja, where Burton Bar (see p056) is the scene in microcosm, although the area is very much in flux. San Sebastián, long the playground of the rich, has a better developed club scene (see p046 and p060). *For full addresses, see Resources.*

Azurmendi

Chef Eneko Atxa describes the dining experience at Azurmendi as 'theatre' and this Michelin-starred restaurant 10km east of Bilbao is certainly a fitting venue for his performances. It was designed by local architects Aterpean as a cross between a warehouse and a traditional farmhouse. You enter the dining room via a vast reception area (above) clad in laminated Douglas fir and lit by Miguel Milá's metallic 'Estadio' ring, which looks almost medieval. Atxa has won Basque Cook of the Year, and applies molecular techniques to Basque classics. Past courses from his superb €55 and €80 tasting menus include roast pigeon with artichoke, and a dish in which the yolk of an egg is supplanted by concentrated squid soup (a 'squegg'?).
Barrio Leguina, Larrabetzu,
T 94 455 8866, www.azurmendi.es

El Perro Chico

Named after the slang term for the coin needed to cross the old toll bridge from here to the Mercado de La Ribera (see p009), El Perro Chico remains one of the best-known restaurants in Bilbao. Since it opened in 1986, it seems that every film star, architect or fashion designer to have visited town has sampled its French take on Basque cuisine. Small and intimate, with original tiles that date from the 1890s, El Perro Chico's cobalt interior is said to have inspired Gehry's 'Bilbao blue'. Chef Rafael García Rossi played football for Cádiz in the late 1980s when they were in Spain's top division, and his cooking is also of premier-league quality. Try the clams with *kokotxas* (fish cheeks), *bacalao* (cod) with aubergine and leek or steak tartare. *Arechaga 2, T 94 415 0519*

La Pizarra

This *pintxo* bar/restaurant is named after its blackboard menu. It's a hotchpotch of elements: chrome counter, wrought-iron stools, wooden shelves, green Plexiglas screens, chandelier-style table lights and extreme sports on telly. Which makes the drawing-room ambience of the restaurant at the back (above) all the more surprising. Pizarra's location on a gallery-lined street next to Windsor Kulturgintza (see p086) is handy for a refuel during a culture spree. Other nearby options include the stylish Kikara (T 94 423 6840), with its veggie and low-cal menu (rare round these parts), and Sua (T 94 423 2292), where fusion-style dishes are grouped by their serving temperature (25, 50, 75 and -2ºC). The oxtail carpaccio with fish tempura and seafood bloody Mary here are excellent. *Juan de Ajuriaguerra 16, T 94 424 6082*

Bitoque de Albia

The closed ranks of the Basque culinary scene got a shock when English chef Darran Williamson won the Euskal Herria Pintxos Championship in 2009. His concoctions at Bitoque draw the crowds, so visit late morning or mid-afternoon to avoid a long wait. Upstairs (above), overlooking the peaceful Jardines de Albia, gold-coloured brick walls and wood floors contrast with monochrome Corian counters. It's an informal space in which to tuck in to the day's specials (scrawled on Perspex boards), perhaps baby squid ravioli served in ink or the prize-winning *maxibon de rabo con sopa de asados* (oxtail sandwich with roast red pepper soup). Lunch and dinner are served in the cosy, colourful basement restaurant, which comes into its own in winter.
Alameda Mazarredo 6, T 94 423 6545, www.bitoque.net

Branka, San Sebastián

On the far western tip of San Sebastián's voluptuous La Concha bay lies the three-floored café/bar/restaurant Branka. Its aesthetics are as refreshing as the sea breeze blowing through Eduardo Chillida's *El Peine del Viento* (Wind Comb) sculptures nearby. Come for Thursday's summer jazz sessions (8.30-10pm) on the roof terrace, with outsized floor lamps and topiary, and book a table for dinner in the restaurant, where the views are just as impressive through the floor-to-ceiling windows. Branka specialises in fish and the *besugo* (sea bream) and *rodaballo salvaje* (wild turbot) are superb. The out-of-centre location attracts the in-crowd, especially at weekends, when Branka is open until 3am and DJs spin nu-jazz and Spanish house. *Paseo Eduardo Chillida 13, T 94 331 7096, www.branka-tenis.com*

La Gallina Ciega

Colloquially meaning 'blind man's buff', the tiny La Gallina Ciega is a whimsical café, tapas bar, restaurant and gallery all in one. Owners Jon Ezkurdia and Koldo Losada have backgrounds in theatre-set design and have created a unique venue, combining the look of a gentlemen's club (tartan wallpaper, wood panelling) with eclectic boho (an Italian glass hen, antique chairs, sculpture). The lounge has just one six-seater table (above), where lunch is served from Wednesday to Saturday. This should be the reason for your visit. There is no menu – the home-style cooking is driven by what is available at the market, although there is an emphasis on fish. But it's so accomplished you will need to book well in advance. One wall is crammed with paintings of hens donated by arty regulars.
Máximo Aguirre 2, T 94 442 3943

Bascook

This 2010 expansion of chef Aitor Elizegi's empire is set in a former salt warehouse revamped by local firm Verno, who added the diaphanous curtains and cube lights. Dishes are made for sharing and come in local, global and veggie options. Try the pork with smoked mash or the asparagus, coffee and macadamia soup. Finish with a gin-and-tonic *golosina* (jelly sweet).
Barroeta Aldamar 8, T 94 400 9977

La Kabutzia, San Sebastián

The bar/club inside the Real Club Náutico is of interest for the architectural heritage of the building. Constructed from concrete and glass in the shape of a boat in 1929, Real Club Náutico was designed by young local architect José Manuel Aizpurúa and Joaquín Labayen and is a tour de force of Spanish modernism. La Kabutzia opened in 1982, named after a local species of fish, and likes to boast about its film festival connections. The website proudly displays photos of stars such as Al Pacino, Ronaldo, Mel Gibson and Antonio Banderas on its dancefloor, most looking like fish out of water. On the mixing decks, it's disco, Latin, pop, house and R&B. Come here for a sundowner to admire the views across the bay, but save the partying for Branka (see p046) or Bataplán (see p060).
Paseo de La Concha, www.lakabutzia.com

Café Boulevard

A local consortium had to step in to save this Bilbao institution, a fixture since 1871. After decades of wear and tear, the marble art deco interior, its mirrors hailing from the 1929 Paris Expo, was on its last legs. The gilded murals, carved woodwork and stained glass have now been restored and in 2010 the Boulevard once again became one of the city's favourite meeting places. Crisply dressed waiters bustle between tables shouting orders above the din – a scene little changed in well over a century. Downstairs, the 21st century intrudes in the cocktail bar Le Boulevard Nouveau, designed by Madrid firm Lab_matic, who added Arne Jacobsen 'Swan' chairs, shiny surfaces and light panels. Unfortunately, as with other, similar spaces in Bilbao, it has been branded to within an inch of its life. *Arenal 3, T 94 679 1752*

Arzak, San Sebastián

Juan Mari Arzak is the godfather of *nueva cocina vasca*. His three-Michelin-starred tavern was built by his grandparents in 1897 and has always been family-run (his daughter Elena is front of house). It was revamped in 2005 – walls are decorated with iron cutlery moulds and the concrete is indented with spoon shapes. Splash out on the €170 *degustación* menu, which might include the frightening-sounding mead and fractal fluid, or the rather more tempting lobster, potato and copaiba, and warm strawberry soup with dark chocolate 'balloons'. Arzak sells a cookbook revealing his secrets, although whether your dinner guests would feel comfortable with you approaching the table with a blowtorch is another matter entirely. *Avenida Alcalde José Elósegui 273, T 94 327 8465, www.arzak.es*

Burton Bar

The haphazard opening hours and rather lackadaisical mien of this live-music bar on Dos de Mayo tend to suggest that it won't be around long. But then that sums up the vibe of this creative enclave, where anything alternative will invariably test the water. Burton's stone walls and cosy mezzanine house a motley collection of secondhand furniture, retro and kitsch objects – we love the plastic shark doing a handstand – and it's a relaxed venue in which to catch local musical talent. Also on Dos de Mayo, check out the art bookshop Anti-Liburudenda (T 94 415 0375), which organises events; Bullitt Groove Club (T 94 416 3036), for films, gigs and DJ sets; and the crafts market on the first Saturday of the month. Romantic bistro À Table (T 94 415 4766) serves French and Basque fare. *Dos de Mayo 16*

Yandiola

Ricardo Pérez scooped plaudits for his *nueva cocina vasca* at Yandiola's original location, and now the restaurant has a fancy address on the second floor of the Alhóndiga (see p037). The interior is by Philippe Starck, who softened the rough brick walls with drapes and burnished cabinets, and arranged velvety, pistachio- and chocolate-coloured sofas and chairs around well-spaced tables. Pérez has won accolades for his *bacalao*, and it is superb here served wafer-thin with black olives and local anchovies. Also recommended is the lamb with truffles, accompanied by a bottle of 2005 Luberri Cepas Viejas. After you've eaten, climb the stairs to the happening rooftop bar for a postprandial cocktail beside a century-old cupola.
Alhóndiga, Plaza Arriquibar 4,
T 94 413 3636, www.yandiola.com

Porrue

An increasing number of neighbourhood restaurants in Bilbao have no menu and simply cook with the produce available that day from independent farmers and the market. Porrue is one of the best of these, thanks to chef Unai Campo, an expert in the Basque art of grilling. Local specialities include razor clams, oysters, mushrooms, turbot and ox. Modern interiors rarely feature in such establishments, but here the L-shaped venue has been turned into a neo-industrial space, with lighting a key element, and Porrue emits a green glow, appropriate given the provenance of your meal. There are only nine tables, so book ahead. Around the corner, the Basque cuisine at Kalaka (T 94 423 5695) is served in an equally well-thought-out setting that features rusted-steel accents and sculpture.
Alameda Recalde 4, T 94 423 1313

Bataplán, San Sebastián
Situated directly on the beach with
a terrace overlooking the sea, this
mainstream club was redesigned
in 2003 by Futur-2. The 1,000 sq m
venue has a 1960s psychedelic sci-fi
feel. With its plastic furniture, pod-like
corridors, curved lines and spherical
lights, it looks like a Kubrick spaceship.
Playa de La Concha, T 94 347 3601,
www.bataplandisco.com

INSIDER'S GUIDE

ION FIZ, FASHION DESIGNER

Local fashion designer Ion Fiz's collections are celebrated for their flamboyance and exquisite tailoring. His diffusion line, Serie by Ion Fiz, is available at Coquelot (Licenciado Poza 33, T 94 441 2350) and prêt-à-porter from his online boutique (www.ionfiz.com). Although work obliges him to spend time in Madrid, he prefers to relax in his home city. 'Bilbao has everything,' he says, 'tradition and modernity, art and culture. It's always a delight to return.'

Fiz likes to breakfast within the elegant surrounds of the Hotel Carlton (see p016) and at weekends he looks forward to brunch at the buzzy, old-fashioned classic Víctor Montes (Plaza Nueva 8, T 94 415 7067). Afterwards, he might go shopping at Persuade (see p036) or Tokyostory (see p080). For tapas, he highly recommends Bitoque de Albia (see p045). 'Its *pintxos* deserve a Michelin star.'

After a hard day, Fiz often unwinds with friends at Bascook (see p048) or Restaurante Arbolagaña (Museo de Bellas Artes, T 94 442 4657) above the park. 'The seafood and mushroom dishes rival the view,' he says. On a night out, he might pop in to art nouveau-style Bar Basque (Astarloa 3, T 94 424 2621) for cocktails or Antigua Cigarrería next door (No 5, T 94 424 8973), where he likes to order oysters and champagne. 'It's got a great atmosphere when there's live music.' But Public Lounge (see p038) remains Fiz's top party venue. 'The design is fabulous and its G&Ts are the best in town.' *For full addresses, see Resources.*

ARCHITOUR
A GUIDE TO BILBAO'S ICONIC BUILDINGS

After falling asleep architecturally for 100 years, Bilbao awoke with a kiss from handsome prince Frank Gehry. The Guggenheim aside, council-driven projects with Pritzker Prize winners at the helm are underway in the northern suburbs, with plans to regenerate the riverside right up to the Getxo estuary. Richard Rogers' Garellano is a complex of 1,150 flats on the site of the former police HQ and fire station, which have moved to Miribilla. Beside this, Zaha Hadid's plan for the Zorrozaurre peninsula, downriver from Abandoibarra, has been scaled down since *La Crisis*, but will still create a brand-new district – renderings evoke a floating pine cone. The first phase will begin in 2012, when the Deusto Canal is extended to create an island, and 5,000 residences will be built at a cost of €150m.

Various smaller-scale interventions have already arrived with a fanfare, notably the Alhóndiga (see p037), the Iglesia de Santa María Josefa (opposite) and the Sede de Osakidetza (see p072). Architecture buffs may want to head to Zamudio to visit Eduardo Arroyo's Guardería Infantil primary school (Barrio Galbarriatu 6), designed as if through a child's eyes, and the contemporary builds in the technology park, such as the terraced volumes of the Labein Tecnalia Building (Parque Tecnológico 700). However, in a city with a history steeped in transport, it's appropriate that the metro (see p075) and airport (see p076) remain real urban success stories. *For full addresses, see Resources.*

Iglesia de Santa María Josefa

The architectural highlight of Miribilla is this concrete church designed by Eduardo Múgica of Bilbao architects IMB, completed in 2008. The triangular nave (overleaf), painted white and simply furnished with pine benches, tapers towards the altar. One wall is inset with rectangular glass panes in religiously significant colours – purple, green and red – an update on traditional stained glass. Similar windows run up the 24m spire, framing a staircase leading up to the belfry. It's only possible to visit the interior during Sunday Mass (12pm and 1pm). Miribilla is serviced by a new Cercanías station, bored 50m below ground and accessed via a vertical metal shaft. There's a nice symbolism – where once were Bilbaíno miners, now are commuters. *Gernika lorategia 3, T 94 466 2662, www.bizkeliza.org*

Iglesia de Santa María Josefa

Bilbao Exhibition Centre (BEC)
Architects ACXT's 450,000 sq m exhibition centre is one of the largest multipurpose venues in Spain. Completed in 2005 at a cost of €530m, the complex triggered the redevelopment of the Ansio-Barakaldo suburb, although the City Hall remains underwhelmed by BEC's financial performance, saying that it has failed to bring in local investment. The main arena, which accommodates 20,000 spectators, hosts concerts as well as theatre and sporting events, and there are six further exhibition halls. Solar panels on the roof increase the building's energy efficiency. The main entrance is marked by the 98m Torre BEC (opposite), which culminates in a brutal, teetering, yet somehow dainty glass-and-concrete box, providing nine floors of panoramic office space.
Ronda de Azkue 1, T 94 404 0000,
www.bilbaoexhibitioncentre.com

Teatro Campos Elíseos

The city's finest art nouveau monument, affectionately known as La Bombonera (Chocolate Box), was inaugurated in 1902 and designed by Alfredo Acebal and Jean Batiste Darroquy. It reopened in 2010 after a six-year renovation, equipped with contemporary facilities and extra seating. The real draw though is the restored décor. The auditorium (opposite) is an extravagant whirl of gilded columns and curving balconies beneath a domed ceiling. The concrete, brick and plaster façade (above) features a highly decorative horseshoe design that looks as if it might be piped-on whipped cream. On the upper floors, a glass extension provides a pleasing juxtaposition of old and new. Sadly the programming leaves something to be desired but does promote Basque artists.
Bertendona 5, T 94 443 8610

Sede de Osakidetza

Architects Juan Coll-Barreu and Daniel Gutiérrez Zarza's HQ for the Basque Health Department was shortlisted for a 2009 Mies van der Rohe Award. It riffs on the adjacent 19th-century blocks by exaggerating traditional elements, such as the tower and recessed top floor, and then loosely wraps the whole thing in a transparent double-glazed skin. The façade of glass panels and aluminium beams, with its crumpled triangles and trapezoids and bulging volumes, gives the impression that the structure is actually inflating. The building is not open to the public but it is the exterior that captivates, throwing up a mosaic of images reflected back from the sky and the street. It's equally commanding when illuminated at night.

Alameda Recalde/Licenciado Poza

Palacio Euskalduna

Federico Soriano and Dolores Palacios' conference venue opened in 1999, looming over the Nervión like an enormous, rusting hull. On the site of a former shipyard, it won an award for the world's best congress centre and its auditorium, which seats more than 2,000, hosts classical concerts, opera and ballet. The 53,000 sq m interior is impressive, the windowless concert hall suspended as if in a light-flooded dry dock, its shell connected to foyers and dressing rooms by steel pontoons. On the third floor, Basque chef Fernando Canales runs the Michelin-starred Etxanobe (T 94 442 1071), which, if you can ignore the stomach-turning décor, is hailed as the best restaurant in Bilbao, with tasting menus that start at €65.
Avenida Abandoibarra 4, T 94 403 5000,
www.euskalduna.net

Metro

Lord Foster's underground burrows out of the city pavements like earthworms after a downpour. The simple concept takes its cue from London's Tube, and the circular form is retained below ground. In a cavernous 160 sq m wide tunnel, platforms are bolted to the sides and mezzanines hang from the roof so the curves are always visible, enhancing the sense of space in an attempt to combat claustrophobia.

Only concrete, steel and glass are used throughout. As Bilbao is so compact, when the metro opened in 1995, locals dubbed it the *centímetro*. They have since warmed to the idea, nicknaming the entrances with an affectionate diminutive – *Fosteritos* (little Fosters). *T 94 425 4000, www.metrobilbao.net*

Sondika Airport
You may well arrive in Bilbao on
a cheap flight, but you get an instant
upgrade as soon as you step inside
Santiago Calatrava's sculptural 2000
terminal. It comprises a series of skeletal
white shells of steel, concrete and
glass, the roof of the vaulted central
hall pointed longingly at the sky. The
building is often likened to an aeroplane
at take-off – it certainly captures a
feeling of movement – although locally
it is known more prosaically as *La Paloma*
(The Dove). While the airport launches
you out of the city with some style, when
you arrive, straight out of customs onto
the outdoor rear concourse, blinking in
the sunlight, you rather feel you've been
spat out the back like dust in an engine.
A proposed railway link to the city centre
will no doubt soothe the experience.
T 90 240 4704, www.aena.es

Auditorio Kursaal, San Sebastián
Rafael Moneo's auditorium and congress
hall resembles two radioactive blocks
washed up on Zurriola Beach. Built in
1999, the pair boast nearly 6,000 concave,
translucent glass panels, and appear to shy
away from each other and hint at the hills
beyond. During the day, dappled sunlight
bounces off the warm cedarwood interiors.
Avenida de Zurriola 1, T 94 300 3000,
www.kursaal.org

SHOPPING

THE BEST RETAIL THERAPY AND WHAT TO BUY

Cristóbal Balenciaga and Paco Rabanne are Basques who went on to worldwide acclaim but, until recently, only food or furniture would have tempted you over a Bilbao shop threshold. Delightful delicatessens, such as Víctor Montes (Plaza Nueva 12, T 94 415 7067), Casa Rufo (opposite) and López Oleaga (Astarloa 3, T 94 423 0333), have been rumbling stomachs for aeons. The city also has an interiors obsession, which stems from the Basques' love of hospitality. Beyond the big-name showrooms, quirky items can be found at lighting store Luz Bilbao (Rodríguez Arias 20, T 94 416 6011), the eclectic Apartamento 23 (Juan de Ajuriaguerra 23, T 94 424 6603) and the treasure trove Tokyostory (Arbolantxa 6, T 94 479 0393), which specialises in pieces from the 1950s to 1970s.

Contemporary fashion arrived fashionably late in Bilbao, which traditionally dressed in navy, Barbour and conservative Spanish brands, sold in Indautxu's 'Golden Mile'. Now, independents such as The Closet (see p087), Cloché (Heros 22, T 94 661 2673) and QBO (Club 2, T 94 431 5532) stock previously hard-to-find global labels and talented Basque designers including Ion Fiz (see p062), Ailanto, Miriam Ocáriz and Marta Terán. Also check out the ethereal work of Catalan star Josep Font (Cosme Echevarrieta 7, T 94 424 4864). Myriad galleries have sprung up near the Guggenheim; and let's be honest, it was art that brought you here in the first place. *For full addresses, see Resources.*

Casa Rufo

This restaurant/deli opened in 1955 and has barely changed since then. There's an extensive selection of wines, liqueurs, oils, vinegars, condiments and conserves gathered from all corners of Spain, displayed on straining wooden shelves, in cabinets, drawers, boxes, baskets and on tables. There's even a stacked mezzanine as every nook and cranny is used in this old-fashioned store. Pick up some saffron, marinated razor clams or the local *txakolí* wine. We also heartily recommend dinner in the cosy back room, surrounded by memorabilia, books and bottle upon bottle of wine. The rustic Álavesan cuisine is superb, notably the foie gras, *trufas* (truffles), *pimientos* (grilled, salted green peppers) and the *chuletón*, a Desperate Dan-sized slab of tender ox chop for two.
Hurtado de Amézaga 5, T 94 443 2172

Alicia Rueda

Basque designer Alicia Rueda's fluid, feminine clothes have long had an appreciative audience in Bilbao, and in 2009 she opened this upmarket boutique, which also stocks her casual D'Alicia diffusion line. The store was styled by Rueda herself and features velvet drapes with witty touches, a circular pink damask seat and gothic wallpaper. Silver cabinets showcase her accessories. Rainbow-coloured dresses in sensual fabrics with bold detailing are the pieces that have made Rueda's name, but her knitwear and coats in primary colours are equally desirable.
Doctor Nicolás Achúcarro 10,
T 94 400 0578, www.aliciarueda.com

Noventa Grados, San Sebastián

Sleek lifestyle boutique 'Ninety Degrees' is a one-stop temple of cool. The neutral display areas allow the stock to shout for itself, from art books and magazines to CDs, jewellery, fragrances, beauty products and both men's and women's fashion. Established labels, including Balenciaga, Rick Owens and Damir Doma, hang beside the work of up-and-coming designers, such as Boris Bidjan Saberi.

Complete your look at the on-site Marcial Muñoz Peluquería hair salon. Rotating monthly installations and exhibitions are enthusiastically launched with gigs or DJ sessions. The rest of San Sebastián's sleepy retail scene has a long way to catch up. *Mayor 3, T 94 342 0760, www.noventa-grados.com*

Alma de Cacao
This creative local chocolatier uses Latin American cocoa to create confections with flavours such as cardamom, green pepper and jasmine, presented in pretty packaging adorned with poems. There are three branches in Bilbao. This one is a converted 1920s jewellers – the pillars remain, while wengewood fittings display everything choc-related, even cologne.
Bidebarrieta 9, T 94 679 0303

Galería Windsor Kulturgintza

The Windsor has been championing Basque art since 1971. The gallery has since branched out to exhibit Spanish and foreign work, while still promoting emerging local talent and vanguards of the plastic arts – from Darío Urzay to Jorge Oteiza, Joan Brossa and Pepe Espaliú. It is all displayed in a clean, simple room, in the design language of contemporary art spaces worldwide, in which a spiral staircase leads to offices on the mezzanine. If you are feeling flush, there are many more galleries along Juan de Ajuriaguerra and on the parallel Henao, as well as antiques at Zulaica (T 94 424 5492) around the corner. *Juan de Ajuriaguerra 14, T 94 423 8999, www.windsorkulturgintza.com*

The Closet

Raquel Rodríguez and Ainhoa Martija opened The Closet in 2008, and it is one of the few places in town where you can pick up hip international labels. The sparse, industrial design of the narrow store is the work of Asier Portillo. Clothes are displayed along one wall of whitewashed stone, with accessories on glass shelves opposite. In-between, a couple of purple ottomans add a splash of colour. You'll find jeans from Twenty8Twelve and Iro, flowing frocks from Olga de Polga and plenty of rock chic, including dresses by the likes of Gestuz and Stouls. There's also jewellery by Patricia Nicholás and Kenneth Jay Lane, and covetable bags and shoes from Ash.
Ledesma 18, T 94 435 2852

SPORTS AND SPAS
WORK OUT, CHILL OUT OR JUST WATCH

Say what you like about the Bilbaínos but just don't say it to their face – they're hard. Basque festivals always involve some kind of macho posturing, whether it's wood-chopping contests, bull racing (Pamplona, Tudela, Zumaia) or rowing competitions in the rough Atlantic breakers. They also invented the fastest game in the world, *pelota* – try to follow the ball at Club Deportivo (see p090). Appropriately, Bilbao's hills and coast offer plenty for adrenalin junkies – mountain biking, abseiling, bungee jumping, potholing and kite surfing (a local passion) can be arranged through firms such as Troka Abentura (Itsasbide 58, Gorliz, T 94 677 4265).

Bilbao has only recently acquired a feminine side. The Spanish chain Metropolitan (Paseo Uribitarte 4, T 94 423 4444) opened a stylish gym in Isozaki Atea (see p015), offering drop-in classes and an extensive hydrotherapy spa, and then there's the lovely pool above the Alhóndiga (see p037), lined by brick arches. Another 2010 arrival was ACXT's huge Palacio de Deportes (Avenida Askatasuna Etorbidea 13, T 94 470 0678) in Miribilla, which is capped with a distinctive green crown that can be seen from the city centre. It houses an 8,500-seat basketball court, a 25m pool and other sports and fitness facilities. Sea dogs should charter a boat from Puerto Deportivo de Getxo (opposite) or perhaps splash out on a yacht, surely the best way to rock up at the San Sebastián film festival. *For full addresses, see Resources.*

Pabellones de Remo y Vela

The Getxo marina is marred by a sprawl of fast-food restaurants, but take a walk along the breakwater to discover this pair of geometric wooden structures built for the municipal sailing school. Designed by Barcelona architects Abar, and Múgica and De Goyarzu, and completed in 2008, the sailing pavilion is the slightly larger of the two, while the rowing pavilion is the taller. Both contain state-of-the-art facilities and substantial boat-storage space. They are encased in an aluminium-mesh fence with a weathered pine frame arranged in horizontal slats. At night, an orange glow emanates from the base of the pavilions, transforming them into light sculptures. Boat rental starts from €100 a day and rises to €1,200 for a 12-person Zodiac.
Puerto Deportivo de Getxo, Muelle Arriluze, T 94 460 1404, www.getxobelaeskola.com

Club Deportivo

Architects GAZ designed the clever glass façade of Club Deportivo, which gives the impression that its floors are rotating. Inside, there's a gym, boxing ring and pool, as well as saunas, a solarium and a hair salon, but the real reason to visit is to watch the Basque game of *pelota*. Matches normally take place at 5pm on Thursdays and Saturdays (www.asfedebi-pilota.com). Similar to squash but with just two walls and a longer court (*frontón*), *pelota* is a game for two pairs, with players using either their bare hands, a leather glove or a wicker basket to propel the ball at speeds of up to 300kph. With the participants dressed in loose, white outfits, it's a mesmerisingly beautiful spectacle, even if you don't understand the rules.
Alameda Recalde 28, T 94 423 1108, www.club-deportivo.com

Plaza de Toros de Vista Alegre

Despite their fierce reputation, Bilbaínos are lazy matadors. They only use their bullfighting arena for one week a year, during August's Semana Grande – if you can afford the hike in hotel prices, this is the best time to visit the city. Otherwise, apart from the odd concert, the stadium lies eerily empty. The neo-Mudéjar design dates from 1882 but the structure had to be rebuilt in 1962 after a fire, under the direction of architect Luis María Gana. There is a small but interesting museum (closed Saturday and Sunday), with costumes, swords, *banderillas* (short spears) and other bullfighting paraphernalia. In the ring, the *corridas* (fights) themselves are rather theatrical and treated with reverential fervour.
Martín Agüero 1, T 94 444 8698,
www.plazatorosbilbao.com

Mundaka

The delightful fishing village of Mundaka, with its narrow cobbled streets and pretty church, is the unlikely backdrop to what used to be Europe's best wave. Just 40km north-east of Bilbao, Mundaka's tiny population was often overrun by beach boys in wetsuits. However, the legendary left break that pros could ride from the harbour 2km across the estuary vanished after dredging in 2003. Environmentalists and surfers were, like, gutted, man, and there is a campaign to reverse the process. For the latest information, as well as lessons, check out Mundaka Surf Shop (T 94 687 6721). In July and August, there is a more leisurely way to cross the estuary – the twice-daily ferry to Laida beach, where you can grab a cold one and a plate of *tigres* (stuffed, breaded and fried mussels).

Campo de Lasesarre, Barakaldo

Until 2004, there was only one football club worth talking about in Bilbao – Athletic, of course. But while the city waits for its new ACXT-designed San Mamés stadium, slated to open in 2015 as part of Zaha Hadid's Zorrozaurre/Olabeaga development, little league Barakaldo FC scored an early goal with a designer ground of its own. Conceived by Nomad Arquitectura's Eduardo Arroyo, this 15,000-seater stadium has a wide-brimmed, angular, serrated roof and its floodlights resemble periscopes. Colour is provided by red, yellow, orange and blue seats, while sunlight reaches interior corridors and staircases through translucent polycarbonate blocks. If only the football were as beautiful.
Paseo El Ferrocarril, T 94 437 1324, www.barakaldocf.com

ESCAPES

WHERE TO GO IF YOU WANT TO LEAVE TOWN

It's only an hour's flight to Barcelona or Madrid and you can drive to France in 90 minutes. But why bother when there's so much to discover in the Basque country? You could travel inland, to the provincial capital of Vitoria, which boasts its own destination art museum (see p102), on your way to the wineries of Álava (opposite) or the stunning 1950 Basílica de Arantzazu (Oñati, T 94 378 0951), the work of the greatest Basque artists of the last century.

Or pootle down the spectacular coast road to San Sebastián, past wild beaches such as Sopelana and the fishing villages of Lekeito and Getaria, home to the Museo Balenciaga (Parque Aldamar 6, T 94 300 4777) and the bucolic luxury of Hotel Iturregi (Barrio Askizu, T 94 389 6134). Perhaps take a detour to the Museo de La Paz (Plaza de Furo 1, T 94 627 0213) in Gernika-Lumo to learn more about its tragic bombing. San Sebastián itself has a legendary status among foodies, who pilgrimage to the three-Michelin-starred restaurants Arzak (see p054), Mugaritz (Aldura Aldea 20, T 94 352 2455), run by chef Andoni Luis Aduriz, and Restaurante Martín Berasategui (Loidi 4, T 94 336 6471), located in the surrounding hills.

The best time to explore is during festival season. You could spend an entire summer travelling from one village fête to another, watching improvised poetry slams, fish soup-making contests and boatmen trying to pull the head off a strung-up greased goose. *For full addresses, see Resources.*

Hotel Marqués de Riscal, Elciego

Rumour has it that Frank Gehry agreed to reimagine this 1860 Álava bodega after a gift of a bottle of wine from his birth year. Whether he drunk it before designing the folded strips of mirrored stainless steel and gold and pink titanium panels that form the roof of this limestone bodega is unknown. The complex comprises the winery, a hotel, two restaurants and the 1,400 sq m Caudalie Vinothérapie Spa, which has a pool and hammam and offers treatments using grape extracts. Some of the 43 rooms, which have angled windows overlooking the vineyard and marble bathrooms, can be on the pokey side, so book an executive suite. Work off the alcohol at the two nearby golf courses or at the Valdezcarray ski resort, 50km away.
Torrea 1, T 94 518 0880,
www.hotel-marquesderiscal.com

Bodegas Ysios, Laguardia

Santiago Calatrava's graceful 2001 Bodegas Ysios sits just outside the medieval town of Laguardia in the heart of La Rioja Álavesa. The most striking feature of this 196m-long single-storey building is its voluptuous roof, which from a distance looks as if it's had a few glasses too many. Like a rippling wave, the shape evokes the mountains behind it, and aluminium panels bounce sunlight in all directions. The horizontal cedar slats of the façade resemble wine barrels, particularly when reflected in the ceramic-lined pools below. You can learn about the wine-making process (tours at 11am and 1pm daily, and at 4pm during the week; €5 including tasting) in its sleek interior. *Camino de La Hoya, T 94 560 0640, www.ysios.com*

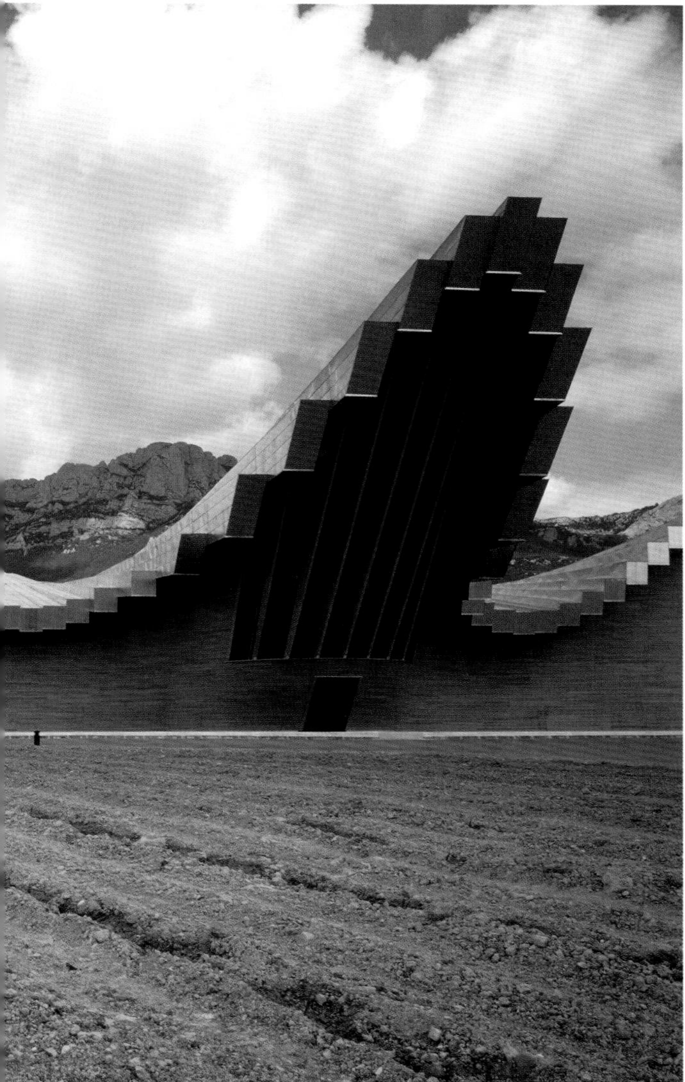

Museo Chillida-Leku, Hernani

This landscaped park, 8km outside San Sebastián, has more than 40 of Eduardo Chillida's abstract, organic sculptures. A 16th-century farmhouse houses more delicate works, many of them eulogies to fellow artists, scientists, philosophers, friends and Mother Nature. Chillida, who died in 2002, worked with iron, concrete, steel, stone and alabaster, and didn't do things by halves – the largest piece here is 56.6 tons – and the immense size gives the sculptures a territorial quality. The prolific artist also has 43 public works located in cities as far afield as Tehran and Washington. Chillida, who himself used to dive through the air as a goalkeeper for Real Sociedad, described his oeuvre as a 'rebellion against gravity'.
Bº Jauregui 66, T 94 333 6006, www.museochillidaleku.com

Hotel Viura, Villabuena de Álava

You wouldn't expect to find such daring design overlooking a 17th-century church in a medieval village 110km outside Bilbao, but this 33-room boutique hotel somehow looks at home. Named after the region's white grape, Viura is the vision of Basque architect Beatriz Pérez Echazarreta and comprises a series of irregular concrete cubes jumbled on top of one another. Each cube is a room featuring floor-to-ceiling windows, with a terrace that offers panoramic views. Bikes are on hand for exploring the area's 42 wineries. We would suggest a visit to Ysios (see p098) and Bodegas López de Heredia Viña Tondonia (T 94 131 0244) in Haro, for its juxtaposition of an 1877 observation tower with Zaha Hadid's futuristic tasting pavilion. *Mayor, T 94 560 9000, www.hotelviura.com*

Artium, Vitoria

Bilbao's cultural renaissance rather put Vitoria's nose out of joint; but the Basque capital hit back in 2002 with a modern art museum of its own. Artium sits in a public square next to the medieval quarter and was designed by the local architect José Luis Catón. Most of the galleries are subterranean and accessed through a shiny white box topped with a shard of glass. The lobby houses Joan Miró and Llorens Artigas' *Mural Cerámico* and Javier Pérez's leviathan *Un Pedazo de Cielo Cristalizado* sculpture (pictured), which consists of more than 12,000 pieces of blown glass hanging from a vibrating sphere. Artium's collection of almost 3,000 pieces focuses on Basque and Spanish art since the 1950s.
Francia 24, T 94 520 9000,
www.artium.org

NOTES
SKETCHES AND MEMOS

RESOURCES
CITY GUIDE DIRECTORY

HOTELS
ADDRESSES AND ROOM RATES

Hotel Carlton 016
Room rates:
double, from €115
Plaza Moyúa 2
T 94 416 2200
www.hotelcarlton.es

Hotel Embarcadero 028
Room rates:
double, from €155;
suite, from €230
Avenida Zugazarte 51
T 94 480 3100
www.hotelembarcadero.com

Gran Hotel Domine 017
Room rates:
double, from €125;
Guggenheim Club Room, from €160;
suite, from €375
Alameda Mazarredo 61
T 94 425 3300
www.granhoteldominebilbao.com

Gran Hotel Ercilla 016
Room rates:
double, from €75
Ercilla 37
T 94 470 5700
www.hotelercilla.es

Hesperia 022
Room rates:
double, from €80;
Junior Suite, from €105;
Presidential Suite, from €190
Paseo Campo de Volantín 28
T 94 405 1100
www.hesperia-bilbao.es

Hotel Iturregi 096
Room rates:
double, from €160
Barrio Askizu
Getaria
T 94 389 6134
www.hoteliturregi.com

Hotel López de Haro 020
Room rates:
double, €195;
suite, from €250
Obispo Orueta 2-4
T 94 423 5500
www.hotellopezdeharo.com

Hotel Marqués de Riscal 097
Room rates:
Grand Deluxe, from €270;
Executive Suite, from €485
Torrea 1
Elciego
T 94 518 0880
www.hotel-marquesderiscal.com

Meliá 016
Room rates:
double, from €105
Lehendakari Leizaola 29
T 94 428 0000
www.solmelia.com/bilbao

Hotel Miró 023
Room rates:
double, from €110;
City Double, from €110;
Junior Suite, from €145
Alameda Mazarredo 77
T 94 661 1880
www.mirohotelbilbao.com

Palacio Urgoiti 026
  Room rates:
  double, from €85;
  Junior Suite, from €175
  Arritugane
  Mungia
  T 94 674 6868
  www.palaciourgoiti.com
Villa Soro 030
  Room rates:
  double, from €135;
  Superior Room, from €175
  Avenida de Ategorrieta 61
  San Sebastián
  T 94 329 7970
  www.villasoro.com
Hotel Viura 101
  Room rates:
  double, from €135
  Mayor
  Villabuena de Álava
  T 94 560 9000
  www.hotelviura.com
Zenit 016
  Room rates:
  double, from €60
  Autonomía 58
  T 94 410 8108
  www.zenithotels.com

WALLPAPER* CITY GUIDES

Editorial Director
Richard Cook

Art Director
Loran Stosskopf
Editor
Rachael Moloney
Authors
Jeremy Case
Mary-Ann Gallagher
Managing Editor
Jessica Diamond

Designer
Lara Collins

Map Illustrator
Russell Bell

Photography Editor
Sophie Corben
Photography Assistant
Robin Key

Sub-Editor
Nick Mee

Editorial Assistants
Ella Marshall
Tanell Pretorius

Intern
Ayse Koklu

**Wallpaper* Group
Editor-in-Chief**
Tony Chambers
Publishing Director
Gord Ray

Contributors
Carmen Gomeza
Alexandra Wicke

Wallpaper* ® is a
registered trademark
of IPC Media Limited

First published 2007
Second edition (revised
and updated) 2011
© 2007 and 2011
IPC Media Limited

ISBN 978 0 7148 6096 1

PHAIDON

Phaidon Press Limited
Regent's Wharf
All Saints Street
London N1 9PA

Phaidon Press Inc
180 Varick Street
New York, NY 10014

Phaidon® is a registered
trademark of Phaidon
Press Limited

www.phaidon.com

A CIP Catalogue record for
this book is available from
the British Library.

All prices are correct at
time of going to press,
but are subject to change.

Printed in China

PHOTOGRAPHERS

Aleix Bagué
Sede de Osakidetza,
pp072-073

Inma Fiuza
Public Lounge, p038, p039

Jeff Goldberg/Esto
Guggenheim Museum,
p012, p013

Roland Halbe/Artur
Campo de Lasesarre,
pp094-095

Iosu Martin
Persuade, p036
El Perro Chico, pp042-043
La Pizarra, p044
Branka, p046
La Kabutzia, pp050-051
Bataplán, pp060-061
Palacio Euskalduna, p074
Metro, p075
Sondika Airport,
pp076-077
Noventa Grados, p083
Galería Windsor
Kulturgintza, p086
Club Deportivo,
pp090-091
Plaza de Toros de Vista
Alegre, p092
Mundaka, p093

Yoann Stoeckel
Bilbao city view, inside
front cover
Puente Vizcaya, pp010-011
Torre Iberdrola, p014
Puente Zubizuri and
Isozaki Atea, p015
Hotel López de Haro,
p020, p021
Museo de Bellas
Artes, p033
Atea, pp034-035
Alhóndiga, p037
Bitoque de Albia, p045
La Gallina Ciega, p047
Bascook, pp048-049
Café Boulevard,
p052, p053
Burton Bar, p056
Yandiola, p057
Ion Fiz, p063
Iglesia de Santa María
Josefa, p065, pp066-067
Bilbao Exhibition Centre,
pp068-069
Teatro Campos Elíseos,
p070, p071
Casa Rufo, p081
Alicia Rueda, p082
The Closet, p087
Pabellones de Remo
y Vela, p089

BILBAO
A COLOUR-CODED GUIDE TO THE HOT 'HOODS

INDAUTXU
Designer fashion labels and global brands rub well-dressed shoulders on the 'Golden Mile'

CASCO VIEJO
Boutiques, *pintxo* bars and tourist restaurants now line the narrow lanes of the old town

GETXO
This fashionable beach playground is one of the most desirable places to live in Bilbao

ABANDOIBARRA
The riverfront fulcrum of regeneration is home to the Guggenheim and plenty more

BILBAO LA VIEJA
A bohemian quarter full of artists' studios, nightclubs and retail and restaurant ventures

ABANDO AND ENSANCHE
The business district has after-work bars, high-quality dining and the main shopping drag

MOYÚA
This upmarket part of town beside the city park boasts boutique hotels and art galleries

MIRIBILLA
The city's newest neighbourhood was built in the last decade on top of a former iron mine

For a full description of each neighbourhood, see the Introduction.
Featured venues are colour-coded, according to the district in which they are located.